CW01021450

THE FUNERAL MASS
READINGS, PRAYERS AND REFLECTIONS

THE
FUNERAL
MASS

Readings, Prayers
and Reflections

VERITAS

Published 2011 by
Veritas Publications
7–8 Lower Abbey Street
Dublin 1, Ireland
publications@veritas.ie
www.veritas.ie

ISBN 978 1 84730 275 5
Copyright © Veritas, 2011

10 9 8

The material in this publication is protected by copyright law.
Except as may be permitted by law, no part of the material may
be reproduced (including by storage in a retrieval system) or
transmitted in any form or by any means, adapted, rented or
lent without the written permission of the copyright owners.
Applications for permissions should be addressed to the
publisher.

A catalogue record for this book is available from the British
Library.

Scripture Readings are taken from *The Jerusalem Bible* © 1966
by Darton, Longman & Todd, Ltd.

Cover design by Lir Mac Cárthaigh, Veritas
Printed in the Republic of Ireland by Paceprint Ltd, Dublin

*Veritas books are printed on paper made from the wood pulp of
managed forests. For every tree felled, at least one tree is planted,
thereby renewing natural resources.*

Preface

This booklet seeks to help you in choosing the readings for the Funeral Mass of a loved one. It also includes a selection of intentions for the prayer of the faithful that you might wish to adapt or use as inspiration when composing your own; reflections; suggested hymns and where they might be sung; as well as instructions on how to conduct the Rosary.

When organising a Funeral Mass, the following will need to be chosen/compiled:

- First Reading – from the Old Testament (or in the Easter season, from Acts of the Apostles or the Book of the Apocalypse)
- Responsorial Psalm
- Second Reading – from the New Testament
- Gospel Reading
- Prayer of the Faithful

Your priest is always on hand to assist and guide you in your choices.

Grateful acknowledgement and thanks is given to
St John the Baptist Church, Clontarf (Prayer of the Faithful) *and*
the parish team in St Conleth's, Newbridge (The Rosary).

Contents

Introduction   8

First Reading
- ◆ Old Testament Readings   10
- ◆ In the Easter Season, from Acts of the Apostles/
  Book of the Apocalypse   16

Responsorial Psalm   19

Second Reading: New Testament Readings   23

Gospel and Gospel Acclamation   32

Suggested Prayer of the Faithful   53

Reflections   55

Suggested Hymns   61

The Rosary   62

Introduction

Adapted from Funeral Rites and Readings,
Brian Magee cm, Veritas, 1995.

In every celebration for the dead, the Church attaches great
importance to the reading of the word of God. A careful
selection and use of readings from Scripture for the funeral
rites will provide the family and the community with an
opportunity to hear God speak to them in their needs, sorrows,
fears and hopes. The readings in this booklet contain the
readings proposed in the Order of Christian Funerals (except
readings 8 and 9 in the Old Testament readings section; all
readings are taken from *The Jerusalem Bible*), and follow the
setting of the readings as laid out therein. It can be used at
home with the family in the selection of readings, in the choice
of readers and their preparation.

These readings speak to all who are present at the funeral
about the meaning of death, about the deceased person and
about all who mourn. They recall us all to an understanding of
death as part of our own lives. It is important that they be read
well. Understandably, the reader may find that the emotions of
the occasion add to the difficulty of public reading. It will help
if he or she has had time to become familiar with the passage
to be read. Many of the texts are familiar, but they will take on
added meaning in the circumstances.

How to prepare
The texts are generally quite short and straightforward. This is a
help if you are nervous, but it does mean that you have to ensure
that the message gets across to those who are listening.

Make sure that you have no problems with pronunciation.
Read the text out loud to get the feel of the sentences.
Remember that you will tend to read too fast, so learn to pause
and control your speech. Be clear about what the main point

of the passage is. Remember that the congregation will be particularly interested on this occasion in what is being said. They will not be so concerned with how you read as with what you are saying.

First Reading

Old Testament Readings

⇒ READING 1

A reading from the book of Job (19:1, 23-27)

Job said:

> 'Ah, would that these words of mine were written down,
> inscribed on some monument
> with iron chisel and engraving tool,
> cut into the rock for ever.
> This I know: that my Avenger lives,
> and he, the Last, will take his stand on earth.
> After my awakening, he will set me close to him,
> and from my flesh I shall look on God.
> He whom I shall see will take my part:
> these eyes will gaze on him and find him not aloof.'

The word of the Lord.

⇒ READING 2

A reading from the book of Wisdom (3:1-9)

The souls of the virtuous are in the hands of God,
no torment shall ever touch them.
In the eyes of the unwise, they did appear to die,
their going looked like a disaster,
their leaving us, like annihilation;
but they are in peace.
If they experienced punishment as men see it,
their hope was rich with immortality;
slight was their affliction, great will their blessings be.
God has put them to the test
and proved them worthy to be with him;
he has tested them like gold in a furnace,
and accepted them as a holocaust.
When the time comes for his visitation they will shine out;
as sparks run through the stubble, so will they.

They shall judge nations, rule over peoples,
and the Lord will be their king for ever.
They who trust in him will understand the truth,
those who are faithful will live with him in love;
for grace and mercy await those he has chosen.
The word of the Lord.

SHORTER FORM

A reading from the book of Wisdom (3:1-6, 9)

The souls of the virtuous are in the hands of God,
no torment shall ever touch them.
In the eyes of the unwise, they did appear to die,
their going looked like a disaster,
their leaving us, like annihilation;
but they are in peace.
If they experienced punishment as men see it,
their hope was rich with immortality;
slight was their affliction, great will their blessings be.
God has put them to the test
and proved them worthy to be with him;
he has tested them like gold in a furnace,
and accepted them as a holocaust.
They who trust in him will understand the truth,
those who are faithful will live with him in love;
for grace and mercy await those he has chosen.
The word of the Lord.

➣ READING 3

A reading from the book of Wisdom (4:7-15)

The virtuous man, though he die before his time, will find rest.
Length of days is not what makes age honourable,
nor number of years the true measure of life;
understanding, this is man's grey hairs,
untarnished life, this is ripe old age.
He has sought to please God, so God has loved him;
as he was living among sinners, he has been taken up.

11

He has been carried off so that evil may not warp his
understanding
or treachery seduce his soul;
for the fascination of evil throws good things into the shade,
and the whirlwind of desire corrupts a simple heart.
Coming to perfection in so short a while, he achieved long life;
his soul being pleasing to the Lord,
he has taken him quickly from the wickedness around him.
Yet people look on, uncomprehending;
it does not enter their heads
that grace and mercy await the chosen of the Lord,
and protection, his holy ones.

The word of the Lord.

➤ READING 4

A reading from the prophet Isaiah (25:6-9)

On this mountain,
the Lord of hosts will prepare for all peoples
a banquet of rich food.
On this mountain he will remove
the mourning veil that is covering all peoples,
and the shroud enwrapping all nations,
he will destroy Death forever.
The Lord God will wipe away
the tears from every cheek;
he will take away his people's shame
everywhere on earth,
for the Lord has said so.
That day, it will be said: See, this is our God
in whom we hoped for salvation;
the Lord is the one in whom we hoped.
We exult and we rejoice
that he has saved us.

The word of the Lord.

⋙ READING 5

A reading from the book of Lamentations (3:17-26)

My soul is shut out from peace;
I have forgotten happiness.
And now I say, 'My strength is gone,
that hope which came from the Lord'.
Brooding on my anguish and affliction
is gall and wormwood.
My spirit ponders it continually
and sinks within me.
This is what I shall tell my heart,
and so recover hope:
the favours of the Lord are not all past,
his kindnesses are not exhausted;
every morning they are renewed;
great is his faithfulness.
'My portion is the Lord' says my soul
'and so I will hope in him.'
The Lord is good to those who trust him,
to the soul that searches for him.
It is good to wait in silence
for the Lord to save.

The word of the Lord.

⋙ READING 6

A reading from the prophet Daniel (12:1-3)

I, Daniel, was doing penance when I received this message from the Lord:

'At that time Michael will stand up, the great prince who mounts guard over your people. There is going to be a time of great distress, unparalleled since nations first came into existence. When that time comes, your own people will be spared, all those whose names are found written in the Book. Of those who lie sleeping in the dust of the earth many will awake, some to everlasting life, some to shame and everlasting disgrace. The learned will shine as brightly as the vault of heaven, and those who have instructed many in virtue, as bright as stars for all eternity.'

The word of the Lord.

⪼ Reading 7

A reading from the second book of Maccabees (12:43-45)

Judas, the leader of the Jews, took a collection from the people individually, amounting to nearly two thousand drachmae, and sent it to Jerusalem to have a sacrifice for sin offered, an altogether fine and noble action, in which he took full account of the resurrection. For if he had not expected the fallen to rise again it would have been superfluous and foolish to pray for the dead, whereas if he had in view the splendid recompense reserved for those who make a pious end, the thought was holy and devout. This was why he had this atonement sacrifice offered for the dead, so that they might be released from their sin.

The word of the Lord.

⪼ Reading 8

A reading from the book of Ecclesiastes (3:1-8)

There is a season for everything, a time for every occupation under heaven:
A time for giving birth, a time for dying;
a time for planting, a time for uprooting what has been
     planted.
A time for killing, a time for healing;
a time for knocking down, a time for building.
A time for tears, a time for laughter;
a time for mourning, a time for dancing.
A time for throwing stones away, a time for gathering them
     up;
a time for embracing, a time to refrain from embracing.
A time for searching, a time for losing;
a time for keeping, a time for throwing away.
A time for tearing, a time for sewing;
a time for keeping silent, a time for speaking.
A time for loving, a time for hating;
a time for war, a time for peace.

The word of the Lord.

⮞ READING 9

A reading from the prophet Isaiah (35:3-6, 10)

Strengthen all weary hands,
steady all trembling knees
and say to the faint hearts,
'Courage! Do not be afraid.

'Look, your God is coming,
vengeance is coming,
the retribution of God;
he is coming to save you.'

Then the eyes of the blind will be opened,
the ears of the deaf unsealed,
then the lame shall leap like a deer
and the tongues of the dumb sing for joy;

for water gushes in the desert
streams in the wastelands

for those the Lord has ransomed shall return.

They will come to Zion shouting for joy,
everlasting joy on their faces;
joy and gladness will go with them
and sorrow and lament be ended.

The word of the Lord.

In the Easter Season, from Acts of the Apostles/Book of the Apocalypse

➤ Reading 1

A reading from the Acts of the Apostles (10:34-43)

Peter addressed Cornelius and his household:
'The truth I have now come to realise,' he said, 'is that God does not have favourites, but that anybody of any nationality who fears God and does what is right is acceptable to him.

'It is true, God sent his word to the people of Israel, and it was to them that the good news of peace was brought by Jesus Christ – but Jesus Christ is the Lord of all men. You must have heard about the recent happenings in Judaea; about Jesus of Nazareth and how he began in Galilee, after John had been preaching baptism. God had anointed him with the Holy Spirit and with power, and because God was with him, Jesus went about doing good and curing all who had fallen into the power of the devil. Now I, and those with me, can witness to everything he did throughout the countryside of Judaea and in Jerusalem itself: and also to the fact that they killed him by hanging him on a tree, yet three days afterwards God raised him to life and allowed him to be seen, not by the whole people but only by certain witnesses God had chosen beforehand. Now we are those witnesses – we have eaten and drunk with him after his resurrection from the dead – and he has ordered us to proclaim this to his people and to tell them that God has appointed him to judge everyone alive or dead. It is to him that all the prophets bear this witness: that all who believe in Jesus will have their sins forgiven through his name.'
The word of the Lord.

Shorter form
A reading from the Acts of the Apostles (10:34-36, 42-43)

Peter addressed Cornelius and his household:
'The truth I have now come to realise,' he said, 'is that God

does not have favourites, but that anybody of any nationality who fears God and does what is right is acceptable to him.

'It is true, God sent his word to the people of Israel, and it was to them that the good news of peace was brought by Jesus Christ – but Jesus Christ is the Lord of all men, and he has ordered us to proclaim this to his people and to tell them that God has appointed him to judge everyone alive or dead. It is to him that all the prophets bear this witness: that all who believe in Jesus will have their sins forgiven through his name.'

The word of the Lord.

☙ READING 2

A reading from the book of the Apocalypse (14:13)

I, John, heard a voice from heaven say to me, 'Write down: Happy are those who die in the Lord! Happy indeed, the Spirit says; now they can rest for ever after their work, since their good deeds go with them.'

The word of the Lord.

☙ READING 3

A reading from the book of the Apocalypse (20:11–21:1)

I, John, saw a great white throne and the One who was sitting on it. In his presence, earth and sky vanished, leaving no trace. I saw the dead, both great and small, standing in front of his throne, while the book of life was opened, and other books opened which were the record of what they had done in their lives, by which the dead were judged.

The sea gave up all the dead who were in it; Death and Hades were emptied of the dead that were in them; and every one was judged according to the way in which he had lived. Then Death and Hades were thrown into the burning lake. This burning lake is the second death; and anybody whose name could not be found written in the book of life was thrown into the burning lake.

Then I saw a new heaven and a new earth; the first heaven and the first earth had disappeared now, and there was no longer any sea.

The word of the Lord.

➤ Reading 4

A reading from the book of the Apocalypse (21:1-7)

I, John, saw a new heaven and a new earth; the first heaven and the first earth had disappeared now, and there was no longer any sea. I saw the holy city, and the new Jerusalem, coming down from God out of heaven, as beautiful as a bride all dressed for her husband. Then I heard a loud voice call from the throne, 'You see this city? Here God lives among men. He will make his home among them; they shall be his people, and he will be their God; his name is God-with-them. He will wipe away all tears from their eyes; there will be no more death, and no more mourning or sadness. The world of the past has gone.'

Then the One sitting on the throne spoke: 'Now I am making the whole of creation new,' he said. 'I will give water from the well of life free to anybody who is thirsty; it is the rightful inheritance of the one who proves victorious; and I will be his God and he a son to me.'

The word of the Lord.

Responsorial Psalm

A word about the Responsorial Psalm. The responsorial psalm may be sung, but if it is to be read, remember that it is a poem and has a musical rhythm. Also, the reader should help the congregation to remember the response by repeating it with them, but should never cue them in by saying: 'Response!' (Adapted from *Funeral Rites and Readings*.)

❧ RESPONSORIAL PSALM 1

Ps 22

Response: *The Lord is my shepherd;*
             there is nothing I shall want.

1. The Lord is my shepherd;
    there is nothing I shall want.
    Fresh and green are the pastures
    where he gives me repose.
    Near restful waters he leads me,
    to revive my drooping spirit. (R)

2. He guides me along the right path;
    he is true to his name.
    If I should walk in the valley of darkness
    no evil would I fear.
    You are there with your crook and your staff;
    with these you give me comfort. (R)

3. You have prepared a banquet for me
    in the sight of my foes.
    My head you have anointed with oil;
    my cup is overflowing. (R)

4. Surely goodness and kindness shall follow me
    all the days of my life.
    In the Lord's own house shall I dwell
    for ever and ever. (R)

⮊ RESPONSORIAL PSALM 2

Ps 24:6-7, 17-18, 20-21

Response: *To you, O Lord, I lift up my soul.*

1. Remember your mercy, Lord,
    and the love you have shown from of old.
    In your love remember me,
    because of your goodness, O Lord. (R)

2. Relieve the anguish of my heart
    and set me free from my distress.
    See my affliction and my toil
    and take all my sins away. (R)

3. Preserve my life and rescue me.
    Do not disappoint me, you are my refuge.
    May innocence and uprightness protect me:
    for my hope is in you, O Lord. (R)

⮊ RESPONSORIAL PSALM 3

Ps 142:1-2, 5-8, 10

Response: *Lord, listen to my prayer.*

1. Lord, listen to my prayer:
    turn your ear to my appeal.
    You are faithful, you are just; give answer.
    Do not call your servant to judgement;
    for no one is just in your sight. (R)

2. I remember the days that are past:
    I ponder all your works.
    I muse on what your hand has wrought
    and to you I stretch out my hands.
    Like a parched land my soul thirsts for you. (R)

3. Lord, make haste and give me answer:
    for my spirit fails within me.
    In the morning let me know your love
    for I put my trust in you. (R)

4. Teach me to do your will
   for you, O Lord, are my God.
   Let your good spirit guide me
   in ways that are level and smooth. (R)

➔ RESPONSORIAL PSALM 4

Ps 129

Response: *Out of depths I cry to you, O Lord.*

1. Out of depths I cry to you, O Lord,
   Lord, hear my voice!
   O let your ears be attentive
   to the voice of my pleading. (R)

2. If you, O Lord, should mark our guilt,
   Lord, who would survive?
   But with you is found forgiveness:
   more than this we revere you. (R)

3. My soul is waiting for the Lord,
   I count on his word.
   My soul is longing for the Lord,
   more than watchman for daybreak. (R)

4. Because with the Lord there is mercy
   and fullness of redemption,
   Israel indeed he will redeem
   for all its iniquity. (R)

➔ RESPONSORIAL PSALM 5

Ps 102:8, 10, 13-18

Response: *The Lord is compassion and love*
   or   *The salvation of the just comes from the Lord.*

1. The Lord is compassion and love,
   slow to anger and rich in mercy.
   He does not treat us according to our sins
   nor repay us according to our faults. (R)

2. As a father has compassion on his sons,
   the Lord has pity on those who fear him;
   for he knows of what we are made,
   he remembers that we are dust. (R)

3. As for man, his days are like grass:
   he flowers like the flower of the field,
   the wind blows and he is gone
   and his place never sees him again. (R)

4. But the love of the Lord is everlasting
   upon those who hold him in fear;
   his justice reaches out to children's children
   when they keep his covenant in truth. (R)

➤ Responsorial Psalm 6

Ps 41:2, 3, 5

Response: *My soul is thirsting for God,*
              the God of my life.

1. Like the deer that yearns
   for running streams,
   so my soul is yearning
   for you, my God. (R)

2. My soul is thirsting for God,
   the God of my life;
   when can I enter and see
   the face of God? (R)

3. These things will I remember
   as I pour out my soul:
   how I would lead the rejoicing crowd
   into the house of God,
   amid cries of gladness and thanksgiving,
   the throng wild with joy. (R)

Second Reading

New Testament Readings

➣ READING 1

A reading from the letter of St Paul to the Romans (5:5-11)

Hope is not deceptive, because the love of God has been poured into our hearts by the Holy Spirit which has been given us. We were still helpless when at his appointed moment Christ died for sinful men. It is not easy to die even for a good man – though of course for someone really worthy, a man might be prepared to die – but what proves that God loves us is that Christ died for us while we were still sinners. Having died to make us righteous, is it likely that he would now fail to save us from God's anger? When we were reconciled to God by the death of his Son, we were still enemies; now that we have been reconciled, surely we may count on being saved by the life of his Son? Not merely because we have been reconciled but because we are filled with joyful trust in God, through our Lord Jesus Christ, through whom we have already gained our reconciliation.

The word of the Lord.

➣ READING 2

A reading from the letter of St Paul to the Romans (5:17-21)

If it is certain that death reigned over everyone as the consequence of one man's fall, it is even more certain that one man, Jesus Christ, will cause everyone to reign in life who receives the free gift that he does not deserve, of being made righteous. Again, as one man's fall brought condemnation on everyone, so the good act of one man brings everyone life and makes them justified. As by one man's disobedience many were made sinners, so by one man's obedience many will be made righteous. When law came, it was to multiply the opportunities of falling, but however great the number of sins committed, grace was even greater; and so, just as sin reigned wherever there was death, so grace will reign to bring eternal life thanks to the righteousness that comes through Jesus Christ our Lord.

The word of the Lord.

➣ Reading 3

A reading from the letter of St Paul to the Romans (6:3-9)

When we were baptised in Christ Jesus we were baptised in his death; in other words, when we were baptised we went into the tomb with him and joined him in death, so that as Christ was raised from the dead by the Father's glory, we too might live a new life.

If in union with Christ we have imitated his death, we shall also imitate him in his resurrection. We must realise that our former selves have been crucified with him to destroy this sinful body and to free us from the slavery of sin. When a man dies, of course, he has finished with sin.

But we believe that having died with Christ we shall return to life with him: Christ, as we know, having been raised from the dead will never die again. Death has no power over him any more.

The word of the Lord.

Shorter form

A reading from the letter of St Paul to the Romans (6:3-4, 8-9)

When we were baptised in Christ Jesus we were baptised in his death; in other words, when we were baptised we went into the tomb with him and joined him in death, so that as Christ was raised from the dead by the Father's glory, we too might live a new life.

But we believe that having died with Christ we shall return to life with him: Christ, as we know, having been raised from the dead will never die again. Death has no power over him any more.

The word of the Lord.

≳ READING 4

A reading from the letter of St Paul to the Romans (8:14-23)

Everyone moved by the Spirit is a son of God. The spirit you received is not the spirit of slaves bringing fear into your lives again; it is the spirit of sons, and it makes us cry out, 'Abba, Father!' The Spirit himself and our spirit bear united witness that we are children of God. And if we are children we are heirs as well: heirs of God and coheirs with Christ, sharing his sufferings so as to share his glory.

I think that what we suffer in this life can never be compared to the glory, as yet unrevealed, which is waiting for us. The whole creation is eagerly waiting for God to reveal his sons. It was not for any fault on the part of creation that it was made unable to attain its purpose, it was made so by God; but creation still retains the hope of being freed, like us, from its slavery to decadence, to enjoy the same freedom and glory as the children of God. From the beginning till now the entire creation, as we know, has been groaning in one great act of giving birth; and not only creation, but all of us who possess the first-fruits of the Spirit, we too groan inwardly as we wait for our bodies to be set free.

The word of the Lord.

➤ READING 5

A reading from the letter of St Paul to the Romans (8:31-35, 37-39)

With God on our side who can be against us? Since God did not spare his own Son, but gave him up to benefit us all, we may be certain, after such a gift, that he will not refuse anything he can give. Could anyone accuse those that God has chosen? When God acquits, could anyone condemn? Could Christ Jesus? No! He not only died for us – he rose from the dead, and there at God's right hand he stands and pleads for us.

Nothing therefore can come between us and the love of Christ, even if we are troubled or worried, or being persecuted, or lacking food or clothes, or being threatened or even attacked. These are the trials through which we triumph, by the power of him who loved us.

For I am certain of this: neither death nor life, no angel, no prince, nothing that exists, nothing still to come, not any power, or height or depth, nor any created thing, can ever come between us and the love of God made visible in Christ Jesus our Lord.

The word of the Lord.

➤ READING 6

A reading from the letter of St Paul to the Romans (14:7-12)

The life and death of each of us has its influence on others; if we live, we live for the Lord; and if we die, we die for the Lord, so that alive or dead we belong to the Lord. This explains why Christ both died and came to life, it was so that he might be Lord both of the dead and of the living. We shall all have to stand before the judgement seat of God; as scripture says: By my life – it is the Lord who speaks – every knee shall bend before me, and every tongue shall praise God. It is to God, therefore, that each of us must give an account of himself.

The word of the Lord.

⤳ READING 7

A reading from the first letter of St Paul to the Corinthians (15:20-28)

Christ has been raised from the dead, the first-fruits of all who have fallen asleep. Death came through one man and in the same way the resurrection of the dead has come though one man. Just as all men die in Adam, so all men will be brought to life in Christ; but all of them in their proper order; Christ as the first-fruits and then, after the coming of Christ, those who belong to him. After that will come the end, when he hands over the kingdom to God the Father. For he must be king until he has put all his enemies under his feet and the last of the enemies to be destroyed is death, for everything is to be put under his feet. – Though when it is said that everything is subjected, this clearly cannot include the One who subjected everything to him. And when everything is subjected to him, then the Son himself will be subject in his turn to the One who subjected all things to him, so that God may be all in all.

The word of the Lord.

SHORTER FORM

A reading from the first letter of St Paul to the Corinthians (15:20-23)

Christ has been raised from the dead, the first-fruits of all who have fallen asleep. Death came through one man and in the same way the resurrection of the dead has come though one man. Just as all men die in Adam, so all men will be brought to life in Christ; but all of them in their proper order; Christ as the first-fruits and then, after the coming of Christ, those who belong to him.

The word of the Lord.

⮞ Reading 8

A reading from the first letter of St Paul to the Corinthians (15:51-57)

I will tell you something that has been secret: that we are not all going to die, but we shall all be changed. This will be instantaneous, in the twinkling of an eye, when the last trumpet sounds. It will sound, and the dead will be raised, imperishable, and we shall be changed as well, because our present perishable nature must put on imperishability and this mortal nature must put on immortality.

When this perishable nature has put on imperishability, and when this mortal nature has put on immortality, then the words of scripture will come true: Death is swallowed up in victory. Death, where is your victory? Death, where is your sting? Now the sting of death is sin, and sin gets its power from the Law. So let us thank God for giving us the victory through our Lord Jesus Christ.

The word of the Lord.

⮞ Reading 9

A reading from the second letter of St Paul to the Corinthians (4:14–5:1)

We know that he who raised the Lord Jesus to life will raise us with Jesus in our turn, and put us by his side and you with us. You see, all this is for your benefit, so that the more grace is multiplied among people, the more thanksgiving there will be, to the glory of God.

That is why there is no weakening on our part, and instead, though this outer man of ours may be falling into decay, the inner man is renewed day by day. Yes the troubles which are soon over, though they weigh little, train us for the carrying of a weight of eternal glory which is out of all proportion to them. And so we have no eyes for things that are visible, but only for things that are invisible; for visible things last only for a time, and the invisible things are eternal.

For we know that when the tent that we live in on earth is folded up, there is a house built by God for us, an everlasting home not made by human hands, in the heavens.

The word of the Lord.

⮞ READING 10

A reading from the second letter of St Paul to the Corinthians (5:1, 6-10)

We know that when the tent that we live in on earth is folded up, there is a house built by God for us, an everlasting home not made by human hands, in the heavens.

We are always full of confidence, then, when we remember that to live in the body means to be exiled from the Lord, going as we do by faith and not by sight – we are full of confidence, I say, and actually want to be exiled from the body and make our home with the Lord. Whether we are living in the body or exiled from it, we are intent on pleasing him. For all the truth about us will be brought out in the law court of Christ, and each of us will get what he deserves for the things he did in the body, good or bad.

The word of the Lord.

⮞ READING 11

A reading from the letter of St Paul to the Philippians (3:20-21)

For us, our homeland is in heaven, and from heaven comes the saviour we are waiting for, the Lord Jesus Christ, and he will transfigure these wretched bodies of ours into copies of his glorious body. He will do that by the same power with which he can subdue the whole universe.

The word of the Lord.

➣ Reading 12

A reading from the first letter of St Paul to the Thessalonians (4:13-18)

We want you to be quite certain, brothers, about those who have died, to make sure that you do not grieve about them, like the other people who have no hope. We believe that Jesus died and rose again, and that it will be the same for those who have died in Jesus: God will bring them with him. We can tell you this from the Lord's own teaching, that any of us who are left alive until the Lord's coming will not have any advantage over those who have died. At the trumpet of God, the voice of the archangel will call out the command and the Lord himself will come down from heaven; those who have died in Christ will be the first to rise, and then those of us who are still alive will be taken up in the clouds, together with them, to meet the Lord in the air. So we shall stay with the Lord for ever. With such thoughts as these you should comfort one another.

The word of the Lord.

➣ Reading 13

A reading from the second letter of St Paul to Timothy (2:8-13)

Remember the Good News that I carry, 'Jesus Christ risen from the dead, sprung from the race of David'; it is on account of this that I have my own hardships to bear, even to being chained like a criminal – but they cannot chain up God's news. So I bear it all for the sake of those who are chosen so that in the end they may have the salvation that is in Christ Jesus and the eternal glory that comes with it.
  Here is a saying that you can rely on:
  If we have died with him, then we shall live with him.
  If we hold firm, then we shall reign with him.
  If we disown him, then he will disown us.
  We may be unfaithful, but he is always faithful,
  for he cannot disown his own self.

The word of the Lord.

≫ READING 14

A reading from the first letter of St John (3:1-2)

Think of the love that the Father has lavished on us,
by letting us be called God's children;
and that is what we are.
Because the world refused to acknowledge him,
therefore it does not acknowledge us.
My dear people, we are already the children of God
but what we are to be in the future has not yet been revealed;
all we know is, that when it is revealed
we shall be like him
because we shall see him as he really is.
The word of the Lord.

≫ READING 15

A reading from the first letter of St John (3:14-16)

We have passed out of death and into life,
and of this we can be sure
because we love our brothers.
If you refuse to love, you must remain dead;
to hate your brothers is to be a murderer,
and murderers, as you know, do not have eternal life in
    them.
This has taught us love –
that he gave up his life for us;
and we, too, ought to give up our lives for our brothers.
The word of the Lord.

Gospel and Gospel Acclamation

➣ READING 1

Gospel Acclamation (Mt 25:34)

Alleluia, alleluia!
Come, you whom my Father has blessed,
says the Lord;
take for your heritage the kingdom prepared for you
since the foundation of the world.
Alleluia!

A reading from the holy Gospel according to Matthew (5:1-12)

Seeing the crowds, Jesus went up the hill. There he sat down
and was joined by his disciples. Then he began to speak. This
is what he taught them:

'How happy are the poor in spirit:
theirs is the kingdom of heaven.
Happy the gentle:
they shall have the earth for their heritage.
Happy those who mourn:
they shall be comforted.
Happy those who hunger and thirst for what is right:
they shall be satisfied.
Happy the merciful:
they shall have mercy shown them.
Happy the pure in heart:
they shall see God.
Happy the peacemakers:
they shall be called sons of God.
Happy those who are persecuted in the cause of right:
theirs is the kingdom of heaven.'Happy are you when
people abuse you and persecute you and speak all kinds

of calumny against you on my account. Rejoice and be glad, for your reward will be great in heaven.'

The Gospel of the Lord.

➣ READING 2

Gospel Acclamation (cf. Mt 11:25)

Alleluia, alleluia!
Blessed are you, Father,
Lord of heaven and earth;
for revealing the mysteries of the kingdom
to mere children.
Alleluia!

A reading from the holy Gospel according to Matthew (11:25-30)

Jesus exclaimed, 'I bless you, Father, Lord of heaven and of earth, for hiding these things from the learned and the clever and revealing them to mere children. Yes, Father, for that is what it pleased you to do. Everything has been entrusted to me by my Father; and no one knows the Son except the Father, just as no one knows the Father except the Son and those to whom the Son chooses to reveal him.

'Come to me, all you who labour and are overburdened, and I will give you rest. Shoulder my yoke and learn from me, for I am gentle and humble in heart, and you will find rest for your souls. Yes, my yoke is easy and my burden light.'

The Gospel of the Lord.

➣ READING 3

Gospel Acclamation (cf. Phil 3:20)

Alleluia, alleluia!
Our homeland is in heaven,
and from heaven comes the Saviour we are waiting for,
the Lord Jesus Christ.
Alleluia!

A reading from the holy Gospel according to Matthew (25:1-13)

Jesus spoke this parable to his disciples:

'The kingdom of heaven will be like this: Ten bridesmaids took their lamps and went to meet the bridegroom. Five of them were foolish and five were sensible: the foolish ones did take their lamps, but they brought no oil, whereas the sensible ones took flasks of oil as well as their lamps. The bridegroom was late and they all grew drowsy and fell asleep. But at midnight there was a cry. "The bridegroom is here! Go out and meet him." At this, all those bridesmaids woke up and trimmed their lamps, and the foolish ones said to the sensible ones, "Give us some of your oil: our lamps are going out". But they replied, "There may not be enough for us and for you; you had better go to those who sell it and buy some for yourselves". They had gone off to buy it when the bridegroom arrived. Those who were ready went in with him to the wedding hall and the door was closed. The other bridesmaids arrived later. "Lord, Lord," they said, "open the door for us." But he replied, "I tell you solemnly, I do not know you". So stay awake, because you do not know either the day or the hour.'

The Gospel of the Lord.

⮞ READING 4

Gospel Acclamation (Mt 25:34)

Alleluia, alleluia!
Come, you whom my Father has blessed,
says the Lord;
take for your heritage the kingdom prepared for you
since the foundation of the world.
Alleluia!

A reading from the holy Gospel according to Matthew (25:31-46)

Jesus said to his disciples: 'When the Son of Man comes in his glory, escorted by all the angels, then he will take his seat on his throne of glory. All the nations will be assembled before him and he will separate men one from another as the shepherd separates sheep from goats. He will place the sheep on his right hand and the goats on his left. Then the King will say to those on his right hand, "Come, you whom my Father has blessed, take for your heritage the kingdom prepared for you since the foundation of the world. For I was hungry and you gave me food; I was thirsty and you gave me drink; I was a stranger and you made me welcome; naked and you clothed me, sick and you visited me, in prison and you came to see me." Then the virtuous will say to him in reply, "Lord, when did we see you hungry and feed you; or thirsty and give you drink? When did we see you a stranger and make you welcome; naked and clothe you; sick or in prison and go to see you?" And the King will answer, "I tell you solemnly, in so far as you did this to one of the least of these brothers of mine, you did it to me." Next he will say to those on his left hand, "Go away from me, with your curse upon you, to the eternal fire prepared for the devil and his angels. For I was hungry and you never gave me food; I was thirsty and you never gave me anything to drink; I was a stranger and you never made me welcome, naked and you never clothed me, sick and in prison and you never visited me." Then it will be their turn to ask, "Lord when did we see you hungry or thirsty, a stranger or naked, sick or in prison, and did not come to your help?" Then he will answer, "I tell you solemnly, in so far as you neglected to do this to one of the least of these, you neglected to do it to me." And they will go away to eternal punishment, and the virtuous to eternal life.'

The Gospel of the Lord.

➤ READING 5

Gospel Acclamation (2 Tm 2:11-12)

Alleluia, alleluia!
If we have died with Christ, then we shall live with him;
if we hold firm, then we shall reign with him.
Alleluia!

A reading from the holy Gospel according to Mark (15:33-39; 16:1-6)

When the sixth hour came there was darkness over the whole land until the ninth hour. And at the ninth hour Jesus cried out in a loud voice, 'Eloi, Eloi, lama sabachthani?', which means, 'My God, my God, why have you deserted me?' When some of those who stood by heard this, they said, 'Listen, he is calling on Elijah.' Someone ran and soaked a sponge in vinegar and, putting it on a reed, gave it him to drink saying, 'Wait and see if Elijah will come to take him down.' But Jesus gave a loud cry and breathed his last. And the veil of the Temple was torn in two from top to bottom. The centurion, who was standing in front of him, had seen how he had died and he said, 'In truth this man was a son of God.'

When the sabbath was over, Mary of Magdala, Mary the mother of James, and Salome, bought spices with which to go and anoint him. And very early in the morning on the first day of the week they went to the tomb, just as the sun was rising.

They had been saying to one another, 'Who will roll away the stone for us from the entrance to the tomb?' But when they looked they could see that the stone – which was very big – had already been rolled back. On entering the tomb they saw a young man in a white robe seated on the right-hand side, and they were struck with amazement. But he said to them, 'There is no need for alarm. You are looking for Jesus of Nazareth, who was crucified: he has risen, he is not here. See, here is the place where they laid him.'

The Gospel of the Lord.

SHORTER FORM

A reading from the holy Gospel according to Mark (15:33-39)

When the sixth hour came there was darkness over the whole land until the ninth hour. And at the ninth hour Jesus cried out in a loud voice, 'Eloi, Eloi, lama sabachthani?', which means, 'My God, my God, why have you deserted me?' When some of those who stood by heard this, they said, 'Listen, he is calling on Elijah.' Someone ran and soaked a sponge in vinegar and, putting it on a reed, gave it him to drink saying, 'Wait and see if Elijah will come to take him down.' But Jesus gave a loud cry and breathed his last. And the veil of the Temple was torn in two from top to bottom. The centurion, who was standing in front of him, had seen how he had died and he said, 'In truth this man was a son of God.'

The Gospel of the Lord.

➢ READING 6

Gospel Acclamation (Jn 11:25-26)

Alleluia, alleluia!
I am the resurrection and the life,
says the Lord:
whoever believes in me will never die.
Alleluia!

A reading from the holy Gospel according to Luke (7:11-17)

Jesus went to a town called Nain, accompanied by his disciples and a great number of people. When he was near the gate of the town it happened that a dead man was being carried out for burial, the only son of his mother, and she was a widow. And a considerable number of the townspeople were with her. When the Lord saw her he felt sorry for her. 'Do not cry,' he said. Then he went up and put his hand on the bier and the bearers stood still, and he said, 'Young man, I tell you to get up.' And the dead man sat up and began to talk, and Jesus gave him to his mother. Everyone was filled with awe and praised God saying, 'A great prophet has appeared among us; God has visited his people'. And this opinion of him spread throughout Judaea and all over the countryside.

The Gospel of the Lord.

⮞ READING 7

Gospel Acclamation (Phil 3:20)

Alleluia, alleluia!
Our homeland is in heaven,
and from heaven comes the Saviour we are waiting for,
the Lord Jesus Christ.
Alleluia!

A reading from the holy Gospel according to Luke (12:35-40)

Jesus said to his disciples: 'See that you are dressed for action and have your lamps lit. Be like men waiting for their master to return from the wedding feast, ready to open the door as soon as he comes and knocks. Happy those servants whom the master finds awake when he comes. I tell you solemnly, he will put on an apron, sit them down at table and wait on them. It may be in the second watch he comes, or in the third, but happy those servants if he finds them ready. You may be quite sure of this, that if the householder had known at what hour the burglar would come, he would not have let anyone break through the wall of the house. You too must stand ready, because the Son of Man is coming at an hour you do not expect.'

The Gospel of the Lord.

⮞ READING 8

Gospel Acclamation (Apoc 14:13)

Alleluia, alleluia!
Happy are those who die in the Lord!
Now they can rest for ever after their work,
since their good deeds go with them.
Alleluia!

A reading from the holy Gospel according to Luke (23:33, 39-43)

When the soldiers reached the place called The Skull, they crucified Jesus there and the two criminals also, one on the right, the other on the left.

One of the criminals hanging there abused him. 'Are you not the Christ?' he said. 'Save yourself and us as well.' But the other spoke up and rebuked him. 'Have you no fear of God at all?' he said. 'You got the same sentence as he did, but in our case we deserved it: we are paying for what we did. But this man has done nothing wrong.' 'Jesus,' he said, 'remember me when you come into your kingdom.' 'Indeed, I promise you,' he replied, 'today you will be with me in paradise.'

The Gospel of the Lord.

➤ READING 9

Gospel Acclamation (Apoc 1:5-6)

Alleluia, alleluia!
Jesus Christ is the First-born from the dead;
to him be glory and power for ever and ever. Amen.
Alleluia!

A reading from the holy Gospel according to Luke (23:44-46, 50, 52-53; 24:1-6)

It was about the sixth hour and, with the sun eclipsed, a darkness came over the whole land until the ninth hour. The veil of the Temple was torn right down the middle; and when Jesus had cried out in a loud voice, he said, 'Father, into your hands I commit my spirit'. With these words he breathed his last.

Then a member of the council arrived, an upright and virtuous man named Joseph. This man went to Pilate and asked for the body of Jesus.

He then took it down, wrapped it in a shroud and put him in a tomb which was hewn in stone in which no one had yet been laid.

On the first day of the week, at the first sign of dawn, the women went to the tomb with the spices they had prepared. They found that the stone had been rolled away from the tomb, but on entering discovered that the body of the Lord Jesus was not there. As they stood there not knowing what to think, two men in brilliant clothes suddenly appeared at their side. Terrified, the women lowered their eyes. But the two men said to them, 'Why look among the dead for someone who is alive? He is not here; he has risen.'

The Gospel of the Lord.

SHORTER FORM

A reading from the holy Gospel according to Luke (23:44-46, 50, 52-53)

It was about the sixth hour and, with the sun eclipsed, a darkness came over the whole land until the ninth hour. The veil of the Temple was torn right down the middle; and when Jesus had cried out in a loud voice, he said, 'Father, into your hands I commit my spirit'. With these words he breathed his last.

Then a member of the council arrived, an upright and virtuous man named Joseph. This man went to Pilate and asked for the body of Jesus.

He then took it down, wrapped it in a shroud and put him in a tomb which was hewn in stone in which no one had yet been laid.

The Gospel of the Lord.

⮞ READING 10

Gospel Acclamation (Jn 3:16)

Alleluia, alleluia!
God loved the world so much
that he gave his only Son;
everyone who believes in him has eternal life.
Alleluia!

A reading from the holy Gospel according to Luke (24:13-35)

On the first day of the week, two of the disciples were on their way to a village called Emmaus, seven miles from Jerusalem, and they were talking together about all that had happened. Now as they talked this over, Jesus himself came up and walked by their side; but something prevented them from recognising him.

He said to them, 'What matters are you discussing as you walk along?' They stopped short, their faces downcast.

Then one of them, called Cleopas, answered him, 'You must be the only person staying in Jerusalem who does not know the things that have been happening there these last few days.' 'What things?' he asked. 'All about Jesus of Nazareth,' they answered, 'who proved he was a great prophet by the things he said and did in the sight of God and of the whole people; and how our chief priests and our leaders handed him over to be sentenced to death, and had him crucified. Our own hope had been that he would be the one to set Israel free. And this is not all: two whole days have gone by since it all happened; and some women from our group have astounded us; they went to the tomb in the early morning, and when they did not find the body, they came back to tell us they had seen a vision of angels who declared he was alive. Some of our friends went to the tomb and found everything exactly as the women had reported, but of him they saw nothing.'

Then he said to them, 'You foolish men! So slow to believe the full message of the prophets! Was it not ordained that the Christ should suffer and so enter into his glory?' Then, starting with Moses and going through all the prophets, he explained to them the passages throughout the scriptures that were about himself.

When they drew near to the village to which they were going, he made as if to go on; but they pressed him to stay with them. 'It is nearly evening,' they said, 'and the day is almost over.' So he went in to stay with them. Now while he was with them at table, he took the bread and said the blessing; then he broke it and handed it to them. And their eyes were opened and they recognised him; but he had vanished from their sight. Then they said to each other, 'Did not our hearts burn within us as he talked to us on the road and explained the scriptures to us?'

They set out that instant and returned to Jerusalem. There they found the Eleven assembled together with their companions, who said to them, 'Yes, it is true. The Lord has risen and has appeared to Simon.' Then they told their story of what had happened on the road and how they had recognised him at the breaking of bread.

The Gospel of the Lord.

SHORTER FORM

A reading from the holy Gospel according to Luke (24:13-16, 28-35)

On the first day of the week, two of the disciples were on their way to a village called Emmaus, seven miles from Jerusalem, and they were talking together about all that had happened. Now as they talked this over, Jesus himself came up and walked by their side; but something prevented them from recognising him.

When they drew near to the village to which they were going, he made as if to go on; but they pressed him to stay with them. 'It is nearly evening,' they said, 'and the day is almost over.' So he went in to stay with them. Now while he was with them at table, he took the bread and said the blessing; then he broke it and handed it to them. And their eyes were opened and they recognised him; but he had vanished from their sight. Then they said to each other, 'Did not our hearts burn within us as he talked to us on the road and explained the scriptures to us?'

They set out that instant and returned to Jerusalem. There they found the Eleven assembled together with their companions, who said to them, 'Yes, it is true. The Lord has risen and has appeared to Simon.' Then they told their story of what had happened on the road and how they had recognised him at the breaking of bread.

The Gospel of the Lord.

⇒ READING 11

Gospel Acclamation (Mt 25:34)

Alleluia, alleluia!
Come, you whom my Father has blessed,
says the Lord;
take for your heritage the kingdom prepared for you
since the foundation of the world.
Alleluia!

A reading from the holy Gospel according to John (5:24-29)
Jesus said to the Jews:
    'I tell you most solemnly,
    whoever listens to my words,
    and believes in the one who sent me,
    has eternal life;
    without being brought to judgement
    he has passed from death to life.
    I tell you most solemnly,
    the hour will come – in fact it is here already –
    when the dead will hear the voice of the Son of God,
    and all who hear it will live.
    For the Father, who is the source of life,
    has made the Son the source of life;
    and, because he is the Son of Man,
    has appointed him supreme judge.
    Do not be surprised at this,
    for the hour is coming
    when the dead will leave their graves
    at the sound of his voice;
    those who did good
    will rise again to life;
    and those who did evil, to condemnation.
    I can do nothing by myself;
    I can only judge as I am told to judge,
    and my judging is just,
    because my aim is to do not my own will,
    but the will of him who sent me.'
The Gospel of the Lord.

⇒ READING 12

Gospel Acclamation (Jn 6:39)

Alleluia, alleluia!
It is my Father's will, says the Lord,
that I should lose nothing
of all that he has given to me,
and that I should raise it up on the last day.
Alleluia!

A reading from the holy Gospel according to John (6:37-40)
Jesus said to the crowd:
    'All that the Father gives me will come to me,
    and whoever comes to me
    I shall not turn him away;
    because I have come from heaven,
    not to do my own will,
    but to do the will of the one who sent me.
    Now the will of him who sent me
    is that I should lose nothing
    of all that he has given to me,
    and that I should raise it up on the last day.
    Yes, it is my Father's will
    that whoever sees the Son and believes in him
    shall have eternal life,
    and that I shall raise him up on the last day.'

The Gospel of the Lord.

⇒ READING 13

Gospel Acclamation (Jn 6:51-52)

Alleluia, alleluia!
I am the living bread
which has come down from heaven,
says the Lord.
Anyone who eats this bread
will live for ever.
Alleluia!

A reading from the holy Gospel according to John (6:51-58)

Jesus said to the crowd:
    'I am the living bread which has come down from heaven.
    Anyone who eats this bread will live for ever;
    and the bread that I shall give
    is my flesh, for the life of the world.'
Then the Jews started arguing with one another: 'How can
this man give us his flesh to eat?' they said. Jesus replied:
    'I tell you most solemnly,
    if you do not eat the flesh of the Son of Man
    and drink his blood,
    you will not have life in you.
    Anyone who does eat my flesh and drink my blood
    has eternal life,
    and I shall raise him up on the last day.
    For my flesh is real food
    and my blood is real drink.
    He who eats my flesh and drinks my blood
    lives in me,
    and I live in him.
    As I, who am sent by the living Father,
    myself draw life from the Father,
    so whoever eats me will draw life from me.
    This is the bread come down from heaven;
    not like the bread our ancestors ate:
    they are dead,
    but anyone who eats this bread will live for ever.'
The Gospel of the Lord.

➤ READING 14

Gospel Acclamation (Jn 11:25, 26)

Alleluia, alleluia!
I am the resurrection and the life,
says the Lord,
whoever believes in me will never die.
Alleluia!

A reading from the holy Gospel according to John (11:17-27)

On arriving at Bethany, Jesus found that Lazarus had been in the tomb for four days already. Bethany is only about two miles from Jerusalem, and many Jews had come to Martha and Mary to sympathise with them over their brother. When Martha heard that Jesus had come she went to meet him. Mary remained sitting in the house. Martha said to Jesus, 'If you had been here, my brother would not have died, but I know that, even now, whatever you ask of God, he will grant you'. 'Your brother,' said Jesus to her, 'will rise again.' Martha said, 'I know he will rise again at the resurrection on the last day'. Jesus said:

'I am the resurrection and the life.
If anyone believes in me, even though he dies he will live,
and whoever lives and believes in me
will never die.
Do you believe this?'

'Yes, Lord,' she said, 'I believe that you are the Christ, the Son of God, the one who was to come into this world.'

The Gospel of the Lord.

SHORTER FORM

A reading from the holy Gospel according to John (11:21-27)

Martha said to Jesus, 'If you had been here, my brother would not have died, but I know that, even now, whatever you ask of God, he will grant you'. 'Your brother,' said Jesus to her, 'will rise again.' Martha said, 'I know he will rise again at the resurrection on the last day'. Jesus said:

'I am the resurrection and the life.
If anyone believes in me, even though he dies he will live,
and whoever lives and believes in me
will never die.
Do you believe this?'

'Yes, Lord,' she said, 'I believe that you are the Christ, the Son of God, the one who was to come into this world.'

The Gospel of the Lord.

≫ READING 15

Gospel Acclamation (Jn 3:16)

Alleluia, alleluia!
God loved the world so much
that he gave his only Son;
everyone who believes in him has eternal life.
Alleluia!

A reading from the holy Gospel according to John (11:32-45)

Mary the sister of Lazarus went to Jesus, and as soon as she saw him she threw herself at his feet, saying, 'Lord, if you had been here, my brother would not have died.' At the sight of her tears, and those of the Jews who followed her, Jesus said in great distress, with a sigh that came straight from the heart, 'Where have you put him?' They said, 'Lord, come and see'. Jesus wept; and the Jews said, 'See how much he loved him!' But there were some who remarked, 'He opened the eyes of the blind man, could he not have prevented this man's death?' Still sighing, Jesus reached the tomb: it was a cave with a stone to close the opening. Jesus said, 'Take the stone away.' Martha said to him, 'Lord, by now he will smell; this is the fourth day.' Jesus replied, 'Have I not told you that if you believe you will see the glory of God?' So they took away the stone. Then Jesus lifted up his eyes and said:
    'Father, I thank you for hearing my prayer.
    I know indeed that you always hear me,
      but I speak
    for the sake of all these who stand round me,
      so that they may believe it was you who sent me.'
When he had said this, he cried in a loud voice, 'Lazarus, here! Come out!' The dead man came out, his feet and hands bound with bands of stuff and a cloth round his face. Jesus said to them, 'Unbind him, let him go free.'
        Many of the Jews who had come to visit Mary and had seen what he did believed in him.
The Gospel of the Lord.

⮑ READING 16

Gospel Acclamation (Apoc 14:13)

Alleluia, alleluia!
Happy are those who die in the Lord!
Now they can rest for ever after their work,
since their good deeds go with them.
Alleluia!

A reading from the holy Gospel according to John (12:23-28)

Jesus said to his disciples:
   'Now the hour has come
   for the Son of Man to be glorified.
   I tell you, most solemnly,
   unless a wheat grain falls on the ground and dies,
   it remains only a single grain;
   but if it dies,
   it yields a rich harvest.
   Anyone who loves his life loses it;
   anyone who hates his life in this world
   will keep it for the eternal life.
   If a man serves me, he must follow me,
   wherever I am, my servant will be there too.
   If anyone serves me, my Father will honour him.
   Now my soul is troubled.
   What shall I say:
   Father, save me from this hour?
   But it is for this very reason that I have come to this hour.
   Father, glorify your name!'
A voice came from heaven, 'I have glorified it, and I will
glorify it again.'

The Gospel of the Lord.

Shorter form

A reading from the holy Gospel according to John (12:23-26)

Jesus said to his disciples:
   'Now the hour has come
   for the Son of Man to be glorified.
   I tell you, most solemnly,
   unless a wheat grain falls on the ground and dies,
   it remains only a single grain;
   but if it dies,
   it yields a rich harvest.
   Anyone who loves his life loses it;
   anyone who hates his life in this world
   will keep it for the eternal life.
   If a man serves me, he must follow me,
   wherever I am, my servant will be there too.
   If anyone serves me, my Father will honour him.

The Gospel of the Lord.

➢ Reading 17

Gospel Acclamation (Jn 6:40)

Alleluia, alleluia!
It is my Father's will, says the Lord,
that whoever believes in the Son
shall have eternal life,
and that I shall raise him up on the last day.
Alleluia!

A reading from the holy Gospel according to John (14:1-6)

Jesus said to his disciples:
   'Do not let your hearts be troubled.
   Trust in God still, and trust in me.
   There are many rooms in my Father's house;
   if there were not, I should have told you.
   I am going now to prepare a place for you,
   and after I have gone and prepared you a place,
   I shall return to take you with me;
   so that where I am

you may be too.
You know the way to the place where I am going.'
Thomas said, 'Lord, we do not know where you are going, so
how can we know the way?' Jesus said:
'I am the Way, the Truth and the Life.
No one can come to the Father except through me.'
The Gospel of the Lord.

➤ Reading 18

Gospel Acclamation (Jn 6:39)

Alleluia, alleluia!
It is my Father's will, says the Lord,
that I shall lose nothing
of all that he has given to me,
and that I should raise it up on the last day.
Alleluia!

A reading from the holy Gospel according to John (17:24-26)

Jesus raised his eyes to heaven and said:
'Father,
I want those you have given me
to be with you where I am,
so that they may always see the glory
you have given me
because you loved me
before the foundation of the world.
Father, Righteous One,
the world has not known you,
but I have known you,
and these have known
that you have sent me.
I have made your name known to them
and will continue to make it known
so that the love with which you loved me may be in them,
and so that I may be in them.
The Gospel of the Lord.

➤ READING 19

Gospel Acclamation (Jn 11:25, 26)

Alleluia, alleluia!
I am the resurrection and the life,
says the Lord,
whoever believes in me will never die.
Alleluia!

A reading from the holy Gospel according to John (19:17-18, 25-30)

Carrying his own cross, Jesus went out of the city to the place of the skull or, as it was called in Hebrew, Golgotha, where they crucified him with two others, one on either side with Jesus in the middle.

Near the cross of Jesus stood his mother and his mother's sister, Mary the wife of Clopas, and Mary of Magdala. Seeing his mother and the disciple he loved standing near to her, Jesus said to his mother, 'Woman, this is your son'. Then to the disciple he said, 'This is your mother'.

After this, Jesus knew that everything had now been completed, and to fulfil the scripture perfectly he said:

'I am thirsty.'

A jar full of vinegar stood there, so putting a sponge soaked in the vinegar on a hyssop stick they held it up to his mouth. After Jesus had taken the vinegar he said, 'It is accomplished'; and bowing his head he gave up his spirit.

It was Preparation Day, and to prevent the bodies remaining on the cross during sabbath – since that sabbath was a day of special solemnity – the Jews asked Pilate to have the legs broken and the bodies taken away. Consequently the soldiers came and broke the legs of the first man who had been crucified with him and then of the other. When they came to Jesus, they found he was already dead, and so instead of breaking his legs one of the soldiers pierced his side with a lance; and immediately there came out blood and water. This is the evidence of one who saw it – trustworthy evidence, and he knows he speaks the truth – and he gives it so that you may believe as well. Because all this happened to fulfil the words of scripture:

Not one bone of his will be broken;

and again, in another place scripture says:

They will look on the one whom they have pierced.

After this, Joseph of Arimathaea, who was a disciple of Jesus – though a secret one because he was afraid of the Jews – asked Pilate to let him remove the body of Jesus. Pilate gave permission, so they came and took it away. Nicodemus came as well – the same one who had first come to Jesus at night-time – and he brought a mixture of myrrh and aloes weighing about a hundred pounds.

The Gospel of the Lord.

Suggested Prayer of the Faithful

Below are suggestions that relate directly to the departed, to the family and friends of the departed, and to those suffering from ill health. Intentions for the needs of the Church, society, and for those in need are also appropriate.

1. We pray for N. In baptism he/she was given the pledge of eternal life. May he/she now be admitted to the company of the saints. *Lord, hear us.*

2. We pray in thanksgiving for all the blessings that came to so many people through the life of N. May he/she now receive the fullness of God's blessings in eternity. *Lord, hear us.*

3. God, you are full of mercy and compassion. Forgive N. any sins he/she committed through human weakness. *Lord, hear us.*

4. N. touched all our lives. Help us to keep alive the values and the ideals he/she put before us. *Lord, hear us.*

5. We pray for all our departed brothers and sisters. Today we pray for … May N. be reunited with them in God's kingdom where there is no more pain or suffering. *Lord, hear us.*

6. We pray for the family and friends of N. In these difficult days may the Lord be their strength and their consolation. *Lord, hear us.*

7. May the God of all consolation be with all who are in sorrow and mourning the loss of N. May he give them the courage and strength to live through this time of suffering which has been laid upon them and give them a deep peace, which only he can give. *Lord, hear us.*

8. Today we are saddened by the loss of one whom we have loved; may our hope in the Resurrection and the promise of eternal life bring us comfort and turn our sadness to joy. *Lord, hear us.*

9. We pray for all who are gathered here in worship. May our own lives bear witness to the generous love of the Lord who lived, died and rose from the dead so that we may have life and have it to the full. *Lord, hear us.*

10. God of all consolation, help us in our grief to comfort one another. May we find light in time of darkness, and faith in time of doubt. *Lord, hear us.*

11. We pray for all our deceased relatives and friends. May the Lord bring them into the light of his presence and give them a share in his glory. *Lord, hear us.*

12. We pray for all who are suffering with ill health at this time. May they experience the loving kindness of the Lord in and through all who journey with them. *Lord, hear us.*

13. We ask the Lord's blessings on all those who are seriously ill. Be close to them in their time of sickness, and if it be your will, heal them and restore them to full health again. *Lord, hear us.*

14. We remember today those who are terminally ill. May the Lord be close to them as they enter into the last stage of their journey towards their homeland. *Lord, hear us.*

Grateful acknowledgement and thanks is given to St John the Baptist Church, Clontarf, for the use of a number of these prayers.

Reflections

Celtic Prayer

May God make safe to you each step.
May God make open to you each pass.
May God make clear to you each road,
and may he take you in the clasp of his own two hands.

Providence Prayer

Gracious God,
you surround us all our days.
We walk and work in the light of your world
and sleep and dream in the gentle dark you created.
Now that our working and dreaming are done,
give us rest and a place to call home,
within the great city of your love.
Through Jesus Christ our Lord,
Amen.

Blessed John Henry Newman's Prayer for the Departed (1)

May he support us all the day long, till the shadows lengthen
and the evening comes
and the busy world is hushed
and the fever of life is over
and our work is done –
then in his mercy –
may he give us safe lodging
and a holy rest
and peace at the last.

Blessed John Henry Newman's Prayer for the Departed (2)

O Jesus, lover of souls, we recommend to you the souls of all those your servants who have departed with the sign of faith and sleep the sleep of peace. We beseech you, O Lord and Saviour, that, as in your mercy to them you became man, so now you would hasten the time, and admit them to your presence above. Remember, O Lord, that they are your creatures, not made by strange gods, but by you, the only Living and True God; for there is no other God but you, and none that can equal your works.

Let their souls rejoice in your light, and impute not to them their former iniquities, which they committed through the violence of passion, or the corrupt habits of their fallen nature. For, although they have sinned, yet they always firmly believed in the Father, Son, and Holy Ghost; and before they died, they reconciled themselves to you by true contrition and the Sacraments of your Church.

I Bind Unto Myself Today

I bind unto myself today
the strong Name of the Trinity,
by invocation of the same
the Three in One and One in Three.

I bind this today to me forever
by power of faith, Christ's incarnation;
his baptism in the Jordan river,
his death on the Cross for my salvation;
his bursting from the spiced tomb,
his riding up the heavenly way,
his coming at the day of doom
I bind unto myself today.

I bind unto myself today
the power of God to hold and lead,
his eye to watch,
his might to stay,

his ear to hearken to my need.
The wisdom of my God to teach,
his hand to guide, his shield to ward;
the word of God to give me speech,
his heavenly host to be my guard.

Christ be with me, Christ within me,
Christ behind me, Christ before me,
Christ beside me, Christ to win me,
Christ to comfort and restore me.
Christ beneath me, Christ above me,
Christ in quiet, Christ in danger,
Christ in hearts of all that love me,
Christ in mouth of friend and stranger.

I bind unto myself the Name,
the strong Name of the Trinity,
by invocation of the same,
the Three in One and One in Three.
By whom all nature hath creation,
Eternal Father, Spirit, Word:
Praise to the Lord of my salvation,
Salvation is of Christ the Lord.

Loricum, or Breastplate of St Patrick (fifth century)

Death Is Not The End

Death is nothing at all. I have only slipped away into the next
    room. Whatever we were to each other, that we still are.
Call me by my old familiar name.
Speak to me in the easy way which you always used.

Laugh as we always laughed at the little jokes we enjoyed
    together.
Play, smile, think of me, pray for me.
Let my name be the household word that it always was.
Let it be spoken without effort. Life means all that it ever meant.
It is the same as it ever was;
there is absolutely unbroken continuity.

Why should I be out of your mind
because I am out of your sight?
I am but waiting for you, for an interval,
somewhere very near, just around the corner.
All is well. Nothing is past; nothing is lost.
One brief moment and all will be as it was before,
only better, infinitely happier
and forever we will all be one in Christ.

Henry Scott Holland

We Give Them Back To You, O Lord

We give them back to you, O Lord
who first gave them to us;
yet as you did not lose them
in the giving,
so we do not lose them
by their return …
For what is yours is ours also,
if we belong to you.

Love is undying, and life is unending and the
boundary of this mortal life
is but a horizon,
and the horizon is nothing save
the limit of our sight.

Lift us up, strong Son of God,
that we may see further.
Cleanse our eyes that we
may see more clearly …

And while you prepare the place for us,
prepare us also for that happy place
that we may be with you,
and with those we love forevermore.

Bede Jarrett, OP

Gone Only From Our Sight

I am standing upon the seashore.
A ship at my side spreads her white sails
to the morning breeze and starts
for the blue ocean.

She is an object of beauty and strength.
I stand and watch her until at length
she hangs like a speck of white cloud
just where the sea and sky come
to mingle with each other.

Then, someone at my side says:
'There, she is gone!'

'Gone where?'
Gone from my sight. That is all.
She is just as large in mast and hull and spar
as she was when she left my side
and she is just as able to bear her load of living freight
to her destined port.
Her diminished size is in me, not in her.

And just at the moment
when someone at my side says, 'There, she is gone!'
there are other eyes watching her coming,
and other voices ready to take up the glad shout:
'Here she comes!'
And that is dying.

Henry Van Dyke

Miss Me But Let Me Go

When I come to the end of the road
and the sun has set for me
I want no rites in a gloom-filled room.
Why cry for a soul set free?

Miss me a little, but not too long
and not with your head bowed low.
Remember the love that we once shared,
miss me but let me go.

For this is a journey we all must take
and each must go alone.
It's all a part of the Master's plan,
a step on the road to home.
When you are lonely and sick of heart
go to the friends we know
and bury the sorrow in doing good deeds.
Miss me but let me go.

Edgar A. Guest

Suggested Hymns

It might be noted that a key moment is the song of farewell (e.g. Receive his/her soul) in the commendation that takes place before the body is brought from the church at the end of Mass. As well as hymns, the usual parts of the Mass and the Responsorial Psalm should be sung.

The following hymns are suggested:

Entrance

Christ Be Beside Me
Abide With Me
Be Still
Walk With Me, Oh My God

Psalms

The Lord's My Shepherd
Be With Me Lord
Be Not Afraid
On Eagle's Wings

Communion

Make Me A Channel
You Are Mine
As I Kneel Before You
Nearer My God To Thee
Amazing Grace

Song of Farewell

Receive His/Her Soul
I Know That My Redeemer Lives

Recessional
O Lord, My God
Day Is Done

The Rosary

In times of bereavement, it is customary for the family and friends to gather in prayerful vigil around the loved one who has died. The Rosary is a very old way of praying. In the company of Mary, our Blessed Mother, we ponder upon the great moments of Jesus' life. We can use Rosary beads to help us as we pray.

Leader: Thou, O Lord, will open my lips.
Response: And my tongue shall announce thy praise.

Leader: Incline unto my aid, O Lord.
Response: O Lord, make haste to help us.

Glory be to the Father, and to the Son, and to the Holy Spirit as it was in the beginning,
is now,
and ever shall be,
world without end.
Amen.

Meditating upon each mystery of the Rosary (see below), we pray:
One Our Father
Ten Hail Marys
One Glory Be

The Sorrowful Mysteries

The Agony in the Garden
The Scourging at the Pillar
The Crowning with Thorns
The Carrying of the Cross
The Crucifixion and Death

The Glorious Mysteries

The Resurrection
The Ascension
The Descent of the Holy Spirit
The Assumption
The Coronation of the Blessed Virgin Mary

Hail, Holy Queen

Hail, Holy Queen, mother of mercy, hail our life, our sweetness, and our hope. To thee do we cry, poor banished children of Eve. To thee do we lift up our sighs, mourning and weeping in this valley of tears. Turn then, most gracious advocate, thine eyes of mercy towards us, and after this our exile, shown unto us the blessed fruit of thy womb, Jesus. O Clement, O Loving, O Sweet Virgin Mary – Pray for us O Holy Mother of God, that we may be made worthy of the promises of Christ.

Eternal rest grant onto him/her O Lord, and let perpetual light shine upon him/her. May he/she rest in peace. Amen.

*Grateful acknowledgement and thanks is given to
the parish team of St Conleth's, Newbridge, for use of this piece.*